THE OLD COLONY MENNONITES

THE OLD COLONY MENNONITES
DILEMMAS OF ETHNIC MINORITY LIFE

by CALVIN WALL REDEKOP

Foreword by Everett C. Hughes

The Johns Hopkins Press
Baltimore

FOREWORD

A sect is a religious organization that is at war with the existing mores. It seeks to cultivate a state of mind and establish a code of morals different from that of the world about it and for this it claims divine authority. In order to accomplish this end it invariably seeks to set itself off in contrast with the rest of the world. The simplest and most effective way to achieve this is to adopt a peculiar form of dress and speech. This, however, invariably makes its members objects of scorn and derision, and eventually of persecution. It would probably do this even if there was no assumption of moral superiority to the rest of the world in this adoption of a peculiar manner and dress.

Although, for reasons which he develops, Redekop insists that the Old Colony Mennonites are not a sect, they correspond in every last point to this general description published by Robert E. Park and Ernest W. Burgess in their *Introduction to the Science of Sociology* (p. 872) in 1921. In the years following, a number of theses on sects were presented at the University of Chicago. They were generally written by a member of the sect, but emancipated enough to look with some detachment at the very group in which he had been bred.

William Graham Sumner had spoken of sects and their war with the mores in his *Folkways,* which was published in 1906, but which came, it is said, out of lectures he gave at Yale a good many years before that. The sect pre-occupied American sociologists, probably because so many of them had sought isolation on the American frontier. They were sects in the pregnant sense of the Park and Burgess and Sumner definitions.

In the eyes of the Roman Catholic church all other Christian religious bodies are sects; and by extension of the same distinction, all but the established churches were considered sects in countries with established Protestant churches. When Max Weber visited the United States at the time of the St. Louis

World Fair in 1904, he was struck by the ubiquity and power of Christian sects, notably the Baptists. But they were not at war with the mores; their ways *were* the declared mores of the middle class. Membership in them, he reports, was a prerequisite to success in business and society. A sect, according to Weber, is a voluntary association which one joins by his own will after being accepted by the members; one is born into a church.*

Some of the sects, or denominations, which Weber saw in America had in the past been something like the sects which Park and Burgess tried to capture in their definition. Many sects had, in America, gone from conflict with the world to a powerful position in it. The charism of their founders had been rationalized into effective administration by those who won the battle of apostolic succession. As Park said of the Mormons, the sect "might become the dominant power in the region that it occupies" (*Introduction to the Science of Sociology*) and become something like a nationality. It became sociological dogma to trace the sect from its original state to the respected position of a denomination. What was not done was what Redekop has now done. The sect-denomination cycle and its counterpart, the charism-bureaucracy cycle, did not take account of the case in which the sect would succeed, against all odds, in achieving its isolation and in maintaining its separate way of life through those very centuries of western history in which "the world" has expanded on every possible frontier beyond which a group of people might seek refuge.

The Old Colony Mennonites are those who have succeeded, in their own eyes. Redekop has, with singular honesty and without a hint of cynicism, or even of self-consciousness, given us the results, the side-effects, of the success, and the tremendous costs. For the costs have been tragic, as viewed from "the world." To depart heroically from the world under charismatic leadership is one thing. To maintain the isolation, to enforce discipline—even to the details of pronouncing their own Low German dialect—on succeeding generations is quite

---

* Max Weber, *Gesammelte Aufsätze zur Religionssoziologie,* Vol. I: *Die Protestantischen Sekten und der Geist des Kapitalismus* (Tübingen, 1920), pp. 207–17 *et passim*.

another matter. It is even crippling. For while one may admire the steadfastness of the Old Colony people, they are not a community of saints who capture the imagination. Indeed, they must stifle the spiritual imagination and limit reading and discussion of the Bible to maintain conformity to what have become their traditional ways. It is indeed a battle that Redekop describes, a kind of backwoods guerilla warfare against an ever expanding world. The warriors are beset not by the great sins of "the world," but by backbiting, petty drunkenness, and lusting after rubber-tired tractors.

Redekop has given, along with his vivid account of Old Colony life, a very thorough review and discussion of literature concerning sects. Above all, however, he has broken through the stereotyping that often follows from basing theories on ideal-types, by giving us a real case of the dynamics of maintaining a deviant "social system." It should occur to any reader that other cases of survival, modification, or disappearance would add to our insights concerning the struggle to be different.

EVERETT C. HUGHES

PREFACE

This study presents a world that is "worlds" away from that of most readers; it reveals as well a perspective that is utterly different from that of most Americans, northern or southern. In some ways the Old Colony Mennonites are similar to other groups found today; yet in many ways they are strangely different. During a visit to one of the settlements, a distinguished anthropologist was moved to exclaim, "This is the closest thing to a Shangri-La I have ever seen."

This book has several interwoven strands. It is a history of the Old Colony Mennonites—the first major one in the English language. Further, it is a sociological-anthropological description of the Old Colony. Beyond this it is an analytical work, defining certain concepts and making certain propositions about religious-ethnic minority groups. Finally, it makes some predictions about what may happen to the Old Colony and to other groups which are somewhat similar.

My interest in the Old Colony was awakened when I was casting about for a dissertation topic. Appropriately enough, my ancestry derives from the same Mennonite trunk, though I had not known about the Old Colony until I saw a strange horse and buggy coming over the crown of a hill during a trip through Manitoba in 1947. Later, in 1958, my wife and I spent four months among the Old Colony people there. Using their suggested contacts, we moved on to the more conservative and exclusive groups in Mexico and lived there in Old Colony homes for six months. Since then I have continued my interest in and connection with the Old Colony, having made at least six subsequent research trips to Mexico and Canada, spending over a year among the colonists in this time.

Most of my research in the Old Colony was conducted in the participant observer role. I never was able to allay completely the suspicion that accompanied my "intrusion" into the Old Colony. My research procedure was normally to spend the afternoons and evenings visiting with the Old Colonists, and then to spend the following morning at the typewriter, trying to reproduce, as faithfully as possible, the conversations and observations and data obtained. Over four hundred pages of single-spaced transcription resulted, and these constitute the basic documentation for the descriptive and analytical parts of the book. I have visited the major settlements in Canada and Mexico but have not yet had the opportunity to visit the new settlements in British Honduras and Bolivia.

Numerous persons have contributed to this book. Everett C. Hughes has served as an inspirational model in all my work. Charles P. Loomis provided guidance in the field and was very helpful in extending aid through grants from the Carnegie Corporation and Project W-108, Anglo-Latino Relations in Hospitals and Communities of the U.S. Public Health Service. The American Philosophical Society made possible a second visit to the field. Earlham College, through a Ford Foundation non-Western study grant administered by Jackson Bailey, was helpful in getting the manuscript prepared.

Special thanks are due Ginny Coover, Joyce Jackson, and Rosella Sawatsky, who prepared the various revisions of the manuscript. My wife Freda has participated in the project from the beginning and has provided various types of assistance and encouragement, among them the gift of a son, born while we were living in a village in the Old Colony settlement in Mexico. His birth served to help ingratiate me with the prolific Old Colonists.

Finally, my greatest indebtedness is to the Old Colony itself, which has provided the material for an analysis of a style of life which, though not possible for many, offers considerable food for thought.

There appears to be in most areas of human experience a tendency toward parsimony and efficiency; the best is that which is the easiest and the quickest. The Old Colony is a striking exception to this principle. It seemingly does things the hard way, the wrong way, the opposite way, the stupid way, and often irritates. There are many who ask, "Why must a group be so obtuse?" This is not a simple question. I hope that it will be at least partially answered in these pages.

CALVIN REDEKOP

CONTENTS

TABLES

MAPS AND CHARTS

FIGURES

Following page 82

Chapter 1

AND THEY SHALL
BE MY PEOPLE

Soon after its discovery, America became the home of many minority groups—if not in fact, at least in aspiration. In the early 1500's the persecuted Anabaptists fleeing Switzerland, when asked where they were going, replied, half in jest, "To America." The endless stream of persecuted minority groups that fled to America constitutes a large part of the ancestry of present-day Americans and of their social institutions. It is from this emigration of protest groups and religious sects that America early derived its concept of the pluralistic society— a society in which men of various beliefs, activities, and attitudes had equal rights.[1]

This pluralism is one of the alleged characteristics of which the American is most proud but which is more or less a fantasy, for America is now properly described as a nation of conformity, homogeneity, and intolerance. Even though many people still consider America a land of hope and opportunity for the vast panorama of cultural subgroups, what has happened to many such groups reveals the truth. It is nowhere more dramatically exposed than in the many accounts available today of the disappearance of religious ethnic minorities.

Most of the studies of minority groups that came to America end with the observation that such groups were destined to disappear. The classic work by Charles Nordhoff, for example, describes fifteen utopian communistic societies, not one of which survives to this day.[2] Mark Holloway studies some twenty utopian communities that flourished in America between 1680 and 1880;[3] not a single one exists today. Pauline Young's *The Pilgrims of Russian Town*, a description of the Molokans, was one of the first detailed scientific studies of a

1. Pluralism is discussed in Ch. 8.
2. *The Communistic Societies of the United States* (New York: Harper & Brothers, 1875).
3. *Heavens on Earth* (New York: Library Publishers, 1951).

religious ethnic minority; this group disappeared as Los Angeles spread its tentacles out into rural lands.[4]

As a refuge for minority groups North America has not lived up to its reputation. Instead of being a haven for minorities, America is becoming a conformist society: "A mass society means more than a mere aggregation of people. Only when a collection of persons is subject to the same processes and formed into a homogeneous unit does it merit the characterization. An urban industrial population formed into a homogeneous unit is the prototype of the modern mass society. The United States with 175,000,000 people [nearly 200,-000,000 today] united under a single system, only twenty per cent of whom are engaged in agriculture, is one of the important mass societies in the modern world."[5]

But "mass society" is only a descriptive term for a certain condition; it offers no explanation for the disappearance of the pluralistic structure.

Why have most minority groups disappeared from the American scene? What are the factors and forces that cause religious ethnic minorities to succumb to the larger society's demands? What are the forces within a larger society that destroy a minority? What are the inner dynamics of religious ethnic minorities? What insights can the study of such minorities offer the student of society? A close look at one ethnic minority may be useful in attempting to answer these questions. This book will try to build upon and extend the insights of earlier works which have dealt with the nature of group life and survival.

The Old Colony has managed to survive for almost a hundred years in North America. Throughout its history it has fled from country to country in search of freedom to follow its own way of life, and it has now opened up its fifth frontier in less than two hundred years. The Old Colony is one of

4. (Chicago: University of Chicago Press, 1932). See also Vernon Louis Parrington, *American Dreams* (Providence: Brown University Press, 1947); Robert U. Hine, *California's Utopian Colonies* (San Marino, California: Huntington Library, 1953).

5. Don Martindale, *American Society* (Princeton: D. Van Nostrand Co., Inc., 1960), p. 48.

the few ethnic minorities remaining in America, but its days may well be numbered despite the determination of its members.

The Background of the Old Colony

Altkolonier Reinlaender Mennoniten Gemeinde is the official name of the Old Colony. A branch of the Mennonite (Anabaptist) tradition, the Old Colony did not split from the Mennonite Church in a cataclysmic way, as is generally the case in sectarian movements. Thus a more careful look at its development is required, especially since no account exists which sets forth the conditions under which the Old Colony emerged.

The Mennonite Church, from which the Old Colony came, has one of the richest and at the same time most tragic histories in Western culture. Its roots go back to Switzerland and the early Reformation.[6] A group of young men who had once

6. The standard works for the general reader regarding the origins of the Anabaptists are John Horsch, *Mennonites in Europe* (Scottdale, Pa.: Mennonite Publishing House, 1950); C. Henry Smith, *The Story of the Mennonites* (Newton, Kan.: Mennonite Publication Office, 1950); a German popular history of the Anabaptists by Stephan Hirzel, *Heimliche Kirche* (Hamburg: Friederich Wittig Verlag, n.d.); and a German-language treatment of some of the early leaders of the Swiss Anabaptists by Edmond Diebold, *Folge dem Licht* (Zurich: Gotthelf Verlag, 1945). A very brief review of the basic beliefs and history of the American Mennonites can be found in J. C. Wenger's *Glimpses of Mennonite History and Doctrine* (Scottdale, Pa.: Mennonite Publishing House, 1947); and another brief history by the same author, emphasizing the Anabaptists' faith and resulting persecution, can be found in *Even Unto Death* (Richmond: John Knox Press, 1961). See Harold S. Bender, "Conrad Grebel, The First Leader of the Swiss Brethren (Anabaptists)," *Mennonite Quarterly Review* (hereafter abbreviated *MQR*), X (January, 1936), 5–45; John Horsch, "Rise and Early History of the Swiss Brethren Church," *MQR*, VI (July, 1932), 169–91, and VI (October, 1932), 227–49. See Horsch, *ibid.,* for an account of the basic conflict between the Anabaptists, who maintained that absolute separation of state and church was essential, and the Reformers, who depended on the state for support in effecting the Reformation. See also Franklin H. Littell, *The Anabaptist View of the Church* (Philadelphia: American Society of Church History, 1952).

supported the Zwinglian Reformation in Switzerland found themselves at odds with Zwingli and along with their followers became a rejected and hunted minority. The stories of their subsequent persecution, harassment, torture, and martyrdom have filled volumes, including Thïeleman Van Bracht's well-known book *Martyr's Mirror.*[7] Thousands of Anabaptists (*Wiedertäufer* in German) were burned at the stake or otherwise killed for their faith, which was characterized by belief in the following: (1) separation of church and state in order that the church could be pure and autonomous; (2) church membership based on adult confession of faith and adult baptism; (3) the disciplined life in the church; and (4) obedience to Christ, which required such activities as nonresistance, simplicity, mutual aid, honesty, love, and ultimately suffering.

This persecuted group preached its faith as it was dispersed throughout the land. The movement spread into Germany, Tyrol, and Holland. In Holland, a Catholic priest, Menno Simons, became the leader of the Dutch branch of Anabaptists. He died of natural causes only because of his success in escaping his enemies.[8] Because of limited religious toleration in Holland, some of the Dutch Mennonites fled to West Prussia in 1539. There they ingratiated themselves to some extent by aiding in the drainage of the Vistula Delta; but Prussian toleration was short-lived.[9]

7. (Rev. ed.; Scottdale, Pa.: Mennonite Publishing House, 1951). A classic compendium of some of the accounts of Anabaptist martyrs, the work is still found in many Mennonite homes and serves an important function in perpetuating the "ethnic" nature of Mennonitism.

8. See Cornelius Krahn, "The Conversion of Menno Simons: A Quadricentennial Tribute," *MQR*, X (January, 1936), 46–54.

9. See Horst Penner, "Anabaptists and Mennonites of East Prussia," *MQR*, XXII (October, 1948), 212–25; Horst Penner, "West Prussian Mennonites through Four Centuries," *MQR*, XXIII (October, 1949), 232–45; B. H. Unruh, "Dutch Backgrounds of Mennonite Migration of the 16th Century to Prussia," *MQR*, X (July, 1936), 173–81; Horst Penner, "West Prussia," *Mennonite Encyclopedia* (hereafter abbreviated *ME*) (Scottdale, Pa.: Mennonite Publishing House, 1959), IV, 923. This section is based primarily on the following sources: Horst Penner, "West Prussian Mennonites through Four Centuries," and David G. Rempel, "The Mennonite Migration to New Russia," *MQR*, IX (July, 1935), 109–28.

Since the Mennonites were nonresistant, persecution and harassment continued in Prussia. The Mennonites were not allowed land for expansion due to population growth, and pressure was put on them to enter military service. With their way of life threatened, they considered migration their only recourse. Fortunately, Russia was interested in having settlers; and when Czarina Katherina granted the Mennonites the privileges they demanded, migration began.

In 1789 a total of 462 families left for the province of Ekaterinoslav in the southern Ukraine. There Mennonite settlement at last prospered. By 1875 there were 163 villages numbering at least 150,000 inhabitants. Once again, however, prosperity proved temporary. After about one hundred years of relative freedom and peace, pressure for the Russification of the Mennonite schools and the Russian requirement of military service resulted in a migration to Canada.[10]

Because of the belief in migration as a means whereby freedom to propagate the Mennonite way of life could be achieved, twelve delegates were sent to America in 1873 to investigate the feasibility of emigration.[11] The United States did not prove a desirable immigration land because it was not interested in entering into private contracts with groups of people. The Canadian government, however, was eager to negotiate for a total group and after much discussion entered into a wholly satisfactory agreement with the Mennonites.

The delegation visited Manitoba, where it was offered two "reserves," one on either side of the Red River in southern Manitoba. This land mass consisted of twenty-five townships or over one-half-million acres,[12] one of the most fertile areas in the province. The decision to emigrate was made, and the

10. See E. K. Francis, "The Mennonite Commonwealth in Russia, 1789–1914, A Sociological Interpretation," *MQR*, XXV (July, 1951), 173–82, 200; also E. K. Francis, *In Search of Utopia* (Glencoe, Ill.: The Free Press, 1955), pp. 20–27, 63. These sections indicate the social organization of the Prussian-Russian Mennonites, namely family, village, commune, and colony, to which Francis adds a fourth, the regional *Kirchen-Konvent*, which was actually formed in 1851.

11. Smith, *The Story*, pp. 448ff.

12. Francis, *In Search*, p. 62. This is the best single source for the description of the migration and settlement of Manitoba.

first major migration (to the "East Reserve," the reserve east of the Red River) took place in 1874. The "West Reserve" was settled very soon thereafter, beginning in 1875.[13] (See Map 1 for the Canadian migrations.)

The groups migrating to Canada came from various settlements in Russia, and these intermixed when they settled in Manitoba. After some time, some of the Mennonites in the West Reserve began to be called the "Old Colony Mennonites," to distinguish them from other Mennonites who had settled in the East Reserve and in scattered areas in the West Reserve.

It is alleged that the more conservative and orthodox left Russia first and that those who felt they could maintain their way of life by adjusting to changing demands of the state remained as long as they could.[14] If this is true, we perhaps can identify the motives of the members of the Chortitza settlements (the "old colony," since it was the earliest colony), who were among the first to migrate to Canada, as motives of preservation of the faith.

Regardless of their precise motives for migrating, the crucial factor in the development of the Old Colony in the West Reserve seems to have been a frame of mind, a way of looking at the world, which began to make itself felt. The more orthodox members began to evidence a black-and-white perception of various issues. To be sure, there was no completely homogeneous outlook in the villages of the Chortitza settlements, but these groups seemed increasingly to be characterized by a conservative spirit. One non-Old Colonist who had observed the emergence of the Old Colony recounted what he felt was the earliest evidence of a new schism, one resulting from varying degrees of conservatism:

13. See Ernst Correll, "Canadian Agricultural Records on Mennonite Settlements, 1875-77," *MQR*, XXI (January, 1947), 36-46; G. Leibbrandt, "Emigration of the German Mennonites from Russia to the United States and Canada in 1873-1880," *MQR*, VI (October, 1932), 205-26, and VII (January, 1933), 5-41; Correll, "Mennonite Immigration into Manitoba: Documents and Sources," *MQR*, XXII (January, 1948), 43-57.

14. See Cornelius Krahn, "Old Colony Mennonites," *ME*, IV, 38-39.

A - FT. ST. JOHN
B - FT. VERMILION
C - HAGUE
D - SWIFT CURRENT

E - WEST RESERVE
F - RAINY LAKE
G - MATHESON
H - AYLMER

Map 1. Old Colony settlements in Canada

"The earliest contention in Russia hinged around the singing of old hymns. The older and more conservative people sang the verses according to the noteless and meter-less book [*die alte Weise*]. The more progressive wanted to sing according to the modern designations. The more progressive men walked out of the meeting and joined the Bergthaler group and never came back. This attitude continued to permeate the 'old colony' settlement in the West Reserve in Manitoba, Canada." [15]

There is conflicting evidence about whether the Old Colony settlement was in fact the most conservative settlement in Canada, at least in the beginning. Some Old Colony leaders believe that the agitation to introduce the modern musical score was spearheaded by Elder Gerhard Wiebe, bishop of the East Reserve. He consulted with Johann Wiebe, his nephew and the bishop in the West Reserve, to get his group to change. Johann Wiebe was able to convince his people, but Gerhard could not. An argument then developed concerning what had been done in Russia, and relations became increasingly strained.

Another explanation for the schism is that Elder Gerhard Wiebe had convinced Johann Wiebe to return to singing in *die alte Weise* (the old form). Later Gerhard Wiebe revised his stand and adopted the new form (*die neue Weise*); thus, the difference between the two groups was accentuated. Though the documents to set the record straight do not exist, the tradition behind the schism provides some insight into the nature of the emerging Old Colony.

Another factor which contributed to the emergence of the Old Colony as a self-conscious, identifiable group was the manner of settlement in Manitoba. In Russia, the village organization had included the structuring of the total way of life. The villages were democratically organized; the basic element of order was the married male, who was entitled to a voice in the affairs of the village. The spokesman for the village was the *Schulze,* who was elected by the males in the

15. Material gathered by the author during field research. (The Bergthaler group refers to another Mennonite group, which also migrated from Russia.)

village and served normally for two years. The villages in the total settlement elected an *Oberschulze,* who represented the Mennonite settlement to the Russian government.[16]

Above this secular order, the spiritual leaders ruled with imposing strength. All cases of insubordination and all misdemeanors were handed over to the *Lehrdienst,* which was composed of the bishop and the preachers and which had the authority to confront the miscreant with his misdeed and to demand penance. If penance was not forthcoming, the council could excommunicate the culprit and ultimately ban him from the society.

In Manitoba, on the other hand, the provincial government had divided the province into municipalities, with reeves as the official representatives. In the East Reserve, the Bergthaler group soon adopted the reeve system for two reasons: (1) they were not very concerned about keeping their own organization alive; and (2) they were not able to maintain control because many farmers lived on farms outside the villages. The Old Colony members on the West Reserve saw very clearly the dangers of adopting the reeve system and reacted to keep the village system alive so that they could retain their own social organization. (See Figure 1 for air view of an Old Colony village in Manitoba.)

The third major factor which caused the Old Colony to emerge was its demand for freedom to conduct its own schools. This point had been an issue in the Mennonites' coming to Canada and had been satisfactorily answered by the Canadian government, which granted them the right to direct their educational program, speak German in the schools, and use the Bible as the main textbook.

The East Reserve members, however, were eager to improve the quality of education and accepted provincial help, whereas the Old Colony members were very reluctant to modernize their schools. Contemporary observers suggest that originally

16. For the most complete sociological analysis of the Russian Mennonite village structure, see Francis, "Mennonite Commonwealth in Russia," pp. 173–82, 200. This basic form has continued to be the format for all the Old Colony settlements except in Fort Vermilion, where the families settled on individual farms. This is discussed below.

the "Old Colony had good teachers, who were even called to teach in the East Reserve," but this condition soon degenerated, even to the point at which the prevalent attitude toward education was, "The more learned, the more perverted."

The controversy over the schools extended to other aspects of life in the East and West Reserves. Since people in the East Reserve were continuing to immerse themselves in "worldly" things, a wide division soon developed. The so-called Old Colony (*Altkolonier* in German) took the name *Reinlaender Mennoniten Gemeinde*[17] because most of the conservative villages were in the municipality of Reinland (West Reserve), Manitoba. (The Reinland Mennonite Church is still the official name of the Old Colony in Manitoba and Saskatchewan.) But the group slowly adopted the name of *Altkolonier Reinlaender Mennoniten Gemeinde,* the term *Altkolonier* being added through common usage. The name Old Colony came to be used by outsiders to refer to those people who were loyal to a rigid belief-system and a traditional way of life, and was adopted consequently by the members themselves.

A possible date for the official emergence of the Old Colony is October 5, 1880, when Johann Wiebe called a *Bruderschaft* (general meeting of all male members) to discuss conditions in the Church. It was decided that all those who were willing to adhere to the old practices and beliefs should renew their commitments; those who were not willing to conform to the old way were encouraged to join the Bergthalers.[18]

It can be said with considerable assurance, therefore, that the Old Colony had developed a strong sense of corporate identity to distinguish itself from other Mennonite groups by about the year 1890. Although no conclusive evidence is available, it is proposed that the forming of a Mennonite school association in 1889 and the opening of a normal school in Gretna in the same

17. Walter Schmiedehaus, *Ein Feste Burg ist unser Gott* (Cuauhtemoc, Chihuahua, Mexico: Druck G. J. Rempel, Blumenort, 1948), p. 51. This is the one eye-witness account of the Old Colony migration to Mexico and life then until 1948. There are important documentations in this volume, though the author portrays the Old Colony as basically a German culture group, which it is not. See pp. 26–28 below.

18. Cornelius Krahn, "Manitoba," *ME*, III, 461.

year by the Bergthal Mennonites were crucial events in the parting of the ways of the two groups of Mennonites in Manitoba.[19]

Thus, the Old Colony came into being when sufficient conflict developed to provide the group with a common identification and an inner structure. A common "enemy" without helped to create a strong unity within. An ex-Old Colonist put it this way: "In the minds of sincere people [Old Colony] there is and has always been the concern to keep the evil world out. It is still prevalent. Of course one might disagree with what they consider the world, but they are sincere. They feel that there is a basic issue involved, but they lack a logical and clear verbalization of it. They have a concept that they are a people of God. The biggest problem is that they have not given clear thought to how they are going to preserve themselves." [20] The development of the Old Colony illustrates well a principle that has long been accepted and was classically stated by Georg Simmel: conflict is necessary for the formation of certain kinds of groups and provides the rallying point for the incipient organization.[21]

The Old Colony Migration to Mexico

Before the immigrations Lord Dufferin, Governor-General of Canada, had promised the Mennonites freedom ("Peace at least we can promise you"),[22] but the pressure to have the Old Colony schools transferred to provincial control increased. In those regions where the Bergthal members formed a majority,

19. Francis, *In Search*, pp. 166ff.

20. Material gathered by the author during field research.

21. See Kurt H. Wolff (ed.), *The Sociology of Georg Simmel* (Glencoe, Ill.: The Free Press, 1950), for a discussion of this principle. He says, "On the one hand, the group as a whole may enter into an antagonistic relation with a power outside of it, and it is because of this that the tightening of the relations among its members and the intensification of its unity, in consciousness and in action occur" (p. 91).

22. Francis, *In Search*, p. 80. The school issue, as it affected all the Mennonite groups, is fully discussed in Ch. 7.

they voted to have the schools transferred to provincial control, thereby requesting a levy for school support which was binding upon all living within the district, including the Old Colony members.

The passing of the Manitoba Public Schools Act of 1890 created great uneasiness because it organized Manitoba schools under a department of education. It required instruction in one language (English) as well as uniform standards. This act was amended in 1897 to make possible a bilingual instruction system and to allow rural schoolboards to hire religious instructors if a certain proportion of the members of the district requested it. Though this compromise had been reached primarily to placate the French Catholic element in Manitoba, the Old Colony was determined to use it to full advantage.

The Old Colony was thus able to continue its school system, in which the age of attendance was seven to thirteen for girls and seven to fourteen for boys, and where classes were held for about six months in the year. However, in 1909, under the administration of Manitoban Premier Rodmond P. Roblin (1900–15), it was decided to employ an educational specialist to upgrade the Mennonite schools, which were considered very unsatisfactory. The plan was successful mainly among the Bergthaler group, but the specialist was not able to require the Old Colony to meet the administration's demands, which included primarily instruction in the English language and the study of Canadian history.[23]

During the war period, the bilingual problem, with one of the languages involved being German, served as the source of much of the controversy. The problem was debated in the Manitoba legislature and, of course, in other circles. The issue was closed upon the passage of the School Attendance Act of March 10, 1916, which made English the sole language of instruction and specified that all children were to attend public schools unless the private schools met the requirements of the department of education.

The Old Colony ethnic minority continued to operate its

23. *Ibid.*, p. 176.

own school system but found increasing resistance from the provincial schoolboard. The resistance became tangible with the opening of numerous schools staffed by Canadian teachers in Old Colony areas. Not a single Old Colony child attended! Finally, in 1919, a description of the Old Colony way of life and a petition asking permission to continue to conduct their own schools were sent to the Manitoba government. The eloquent request was denied.[24] (See Appendix A.)

The negative response of the provincial government precipitated serious discussion among Old Colony members about the action to be taken. The Old Colony sectarian philosophy began to manifest itself clearly: "If you give them a little finger, they will take the whole hand"[25] expressed the basic fears of this pressured group. "They were not interested in compromise, for compromise once begun was hard to stop. . . . It was not necessarily the school itself, but the influence of the school which they feared."[26]

The other factor which caused great uneasiness among the Old Colony members was nationalism. Roblin, determined to make all ethnic groups assimilate with the Canadian people, declared in the legislature: "While we welcome all, our duty to British subjects is to see that the children are taught the principles of the British constitution. . . . What we need is to get the youth filled with traditions of the British flag and then, when they are men . . . they will be able to defend it."[27] This nationalistic spirit, though foreign to earlier Canadian political philosophy, can be said to have developed to a large extent at the coming of World War I.

Though Mennonites as a group were freed from military service by terms of the Canadian constitution, they were expected to contribute to the war effort by purchasing war bonds. The less conservative Mennonites co-operated by supporting the Red Cross, only after being assured that the Red Cross was not supporting the war effort. The Old Colony did not co-oper-

24. Schmiedehaus, *Ein Feste,* pp. 61ff.
25. Material gathered by the author during field research.
26. Material gathered by the author during field research.
27. Francis, *In Search,* p. 174.

ate at all. They refused to support the Red Cross, as well as to buy bonds.

Migration had not been forgotten in the meantime. Between 1895 and 1905, approximately one thousand Old Colony members moved to the Osler-Hague area of Saskatchewan.[28] (See Map 1.) In 1905 another group of Old Colony members, about nine hundred persons, moved to the Swift Current region of Saskatchewan, where nine townships were reserved for Old Colony settlements. These movements were motivated not so much by poor relations with the government as by the desire for more land, however.

It was not until the intensification of the school crisis that the Old Colony considered leaving Canada for political reasons. After exploration of possible relocation sites in Mississippi and Minnesota, both of which held no promise, six men— two from Manitoba, two from Swift Current, and two from the Osler-Hague areas in Saskatchewan—were sent to South America to see if land and freedom could be found. The delegation returned without any hope. In the meantime a smaller delegation, one sent to Mexico, had returned with optimistic reports. Thereupon a new group of six representatives was sent to Mexico in February, 1921, to explore the possibilities of emigration. After conferring with the President of Mexico, Alvaro Obregón, they returned to Canada with a letter, written by A. I. Villareal, the Secretary of Lands and Commerce, and signed by Obregón, granting the Old Colony's requests.[29] (See Map 2 for location of Mexican settlements and Appendix B for document.)

After further visits to Mexico, negotiations were finally con-

28. This figure is arrived at as follows: approximately 1,000 Old Colony members had moved to Saskatchewan by 1905; see Leo Driedger, "A Sect in Modern Society: A Case Study—The Old Colony Mennonites of Saskatchewan" (M.A. thesis, University of Chicago, 1955), p. 25. This estimate is based on the fact that there were eleven villages by 1905, and an average village included from fifteen to twenty families. Only a fraction of the Old Colony moved to Saskatchewan. E. K. Francis states that the Old Colony population was 3,946 in Manitoba (*In Search*, p. 257). He admits that this was a loose estimate used by the Old Colony.

29. Schmiedehaus, *Ein Feste*, pp. 69–86.

1 - CASAS GRANDES, CHIHUAHUA
2 - CUAUHTEMOC, CHIHUAHUA
3 - NUEVO IDEAL, DURANGO
4 - FRESNILLO, DURANGO
5 - SALTILLO, NUEVO LEON (NEAREST LARGE TOWN)
6 - TAMPICO, TAMAULIPAS
7 - BELIZE
8 - SANTA CRUZ

*Map 2. Old Colony settlements in Mexico, British Honduras, and
Bolivia*

summated for the purchase of 230,000 acres, at $8.25 per acre, in the state of Chihuahua near San Antonio de los Arenales (later called Cuauhtemoc). This was the "Hacienda Bustillos," owned by the Zuloaga family. The Old Colony Mennonites from Hague, Saskatchewan, in the meantime had sent a delegation to the state of Durango and purchased approximately 35,000 acres of land. This land was situated about seventy miles northwest of the capital city of Durango, near Patos.[30]

The land in Mexico was bought by several groups, or "corporations," in order to satisfy the legal requirements. These "corporations" were made up of only several men chosen to do the negotiating for the Church. The two corporations for the Old Colony in Manitoba were called "Heide-Neufeld and Reinlaender Waisenamt" and "Rempel-Wall and Reinlaender Waisenamt." [31] The Saskatchewan Old Colony established a corporation consisting of two representatives from each village. These three corporations received money from the individual Old Colony villages and forwarded it to the representatives of the Zuloaga family.

The technical arrangements for the migration were handled in a very efficient manner. The *Oberschulze* (later called the *Vorsteher* in the Old Colony) ordered the *Schulze* in each *Dorf* (village) to call a meeting of all families in his *Dorf*. There each family head was to indicate whether or not he wanted to move to Mexico and how much land he wanted to buy. He was then told to place in the *Waisenamt* (see page 66 for description) all the necessary money to pay for his land in Mexico. Because of the favorable rate of exchange and the great difference in the value of the land, most farmers were able to pay cash for their new farms, and many had considerable sums left over.

The migration to Mexico constitutes an interesting study in organized mass migration. In some cases nearly complete village groups sold their land, packed their belongings, and chased their livestock to the rail station for embarking. Despite confusion, conflict, and hard feelings, the migration could not be stopped. On Wednesday, March 1, 1922, the first chartered trainload of Old Colonists left Plum Coulee, Manitoba, for Mexico. On March 2, the next train departed from Haskett, Manitoba. On March 7 and 11, the third and fourth trains left, both from Haskett. At the same time, two trainloads of migrants left Swift Current, Saskatchewan. All six of these trains arrived safely, about ten days after departure, at San Antonio, Chihuahua.

Approximately 5,300 Old Colonists had landed in Mexico by the end of March, 1922, and had begun homesteading on their land. Since almost all of the immigrants resettled in villages which they named after those in which they had lived in Canada, it might be said that the Canadian Old Colony villages were literally transplanted to Mexican soil. Within a year and a half, homes had been built and the first crop harvested.

Approximately one half of the total Old Colony membership of Manitoba and Saskatchewan participated in the migration.[32] The villages they left were typified by the one described below by an Old Colonist: "There were about thirty-two farms in Chortitz before the migration. About ten families remained. Rosen, a Jew, bought up most of the farms at a very cheap price, at about $15 to $25 per acre, and resold them to other Mennonites and later to Old Colony members who returned from Mexico for about $75 to $100 per acre."[33] This profiteering contributed to bad feelings between the Old Colony members who left and those who stayed.

The emigration of approximately half of the members of the Old Colony created considerable confusion in the mother colony. The Church had earlier ruled that no land in the villages should be sold to outsiders without the consent of the *Lehrdienst*. When the great emigration took place, naturally the practice could not be maintained; accordingly, many other Mennonites and outsiders moved into the Old Colony

32. Krahn, "Old Colony Mennonites," p. 41. Francis suggests the total number participating in the migration was 5,500; see *In Search*, p. 192.

33. Material gathered by the author during field research.

villages in Manitoba and Saskatchewan. This influx tended to break up the Old Colony system. The Old Colony Church ceased to function until its reorganization in 1936. (See Appendix C.) The total social structure also broke down in the Canadian colonies. All of the ministers left with the migration, as did the *Vorsteher*. This meant that all records of the Church membership and other documents were taken along. The *Waisenamt* suffered as well: "The exodus of Mennonites left the *Waisenamt* in bad shape. In fact they had intended to close the whole account down, leaving many accounts not settled. When the group left, they gave the books to a Notary Public in Morden called Black. He was to try to collect the bills and send the money to Mexico. He tried to collect some debts but we protested and appealed the decision." [34] The way in which this fund was handled created ill will which can still be noted today. The total group morale and discipline reached such a low point that many felt the Old Colony group that had remained in Canada would not survive.

Instead of succumbing to seemingly imminent extinction, the remaining Old Colony members regrouped and formed a new church. They were encouraged in this by their reluctance to join other churches, by an awareness of the fact that the Mexican government was beginning to make certain demands upon the Old Colony in Mexico, and by the return, soon after the migration to Mexico (as early as 1926), of individual families to Manitoba and Saskatchewan. Thus, in 1936 an election was held at which three preachers and one deacon were chosen. (See Appendix C.)

Had migration really been necessary? Those who had favored it said that it was absolutely essential to the preservation of faith. They considered any counterargument evidence of obstruction and lack of faith. Conversely, many observers felt that the Old Colony could have worked out its problems with the Canadian government, if only the Old Colony had shown less arrogance and more willingness to talk:

> The most tragic thing that happened to the Old Colony was the move to Mexico. They deteriorated so rapidly there, that

34. Material gathered by the author during field research.

they quickly lost the very principles for which they left Canada. They could very quickly have found out that the things they held dear could be retained here much better than in Mexico. It was a sort of stubborn self-righteousness that sent them to Mexico. Before this, the Old Colonists were rich, prosperous, and progressive people. They lost almost everything financially and everything spiritually by moving. Now the Old Colony does not compare with the other Mennonite groups very favorably. They are less honest, though they are on the average no poorer than any other group.[35]

By 1922, as if in reflection of the opposing points of view, there were six Old Colony settlements. The progressive Old Colony, willing to adapt to the changing environment, remained in Saskatchewan and Manitoba. The traditional Old Colonists, who felt that destruction awaited those who remained in Canada, had settled in the Chihuahua and Durango states of Mexico.[36] (See Table 1-1 and Maps 1 and 2.)

The Old Colony that left for Mexico consigned the ones remaining over to the world. They are still hospitable and friendly and will talk about everything but religion. When you talk to them about religion they say, "Do you talk to us about religion? You are the ones that are lost, and we ought to talk to you." They will not talk religion to us. The Mennonites left Canada to stay pure and unmixed with the world. What they predicted would happen has. That is, the Old Colonists here have gone modern; they use cars, dress like the world, go to school and in general cannot be called a people anymore. The Old Colonists in Mexico have retained much of their original character. They did not want to keep pace with the world. They wanted to be separate. These here [in Canada] have gone to school and come back with frizzed hair. The Manitoba Old Colonists are not different from any other Mennonite group. They behave the same and are no better.[37]

35. Material gathered by the author during field research.
36. The traditional Old Colony later included settlements in Alberta and British Columbia.
37. Material gathered by the author during field research.

Table 1-1   Old Colony Migrations

Date of Migration	Name of Settlement	Location of Settlement
1875	Manitoba	South-central Manitoba
1895	Hague-Osler	Northeast of Saskatoon, Saskatchewan
1905	Swift Current	Southern Saskatchewan
1922	Manitoba Plan[a]	Near Cuauhtemoc in state of Chihuahua
1922	Swift Plan[a]	Northern edge of Manitoba Plan[a]
1922	Durango-Hague Colony	Near city of Durango in Durango State
1934–36	Fort Vermilion[b]	Fort Vermilion, Alberta
1936	Nord Plan[a]	Northeast edge of Manitoba Plan[a]
1940	Burns Lake[b]	Burns Lake, British Columbia
1944	Potosi-Saltillo[e]	Neuvo Leon State
1955	Matheson[b]	Matheson, Ontario
1957	Aylmer[b]	Aylmer, Ontario
1958	Tampico	Tampico, Tamaulipas
1958	British Honduras	Northwest corner of British Honduras (Orange Walk)
1960	Rainy River[b]	Rainy River, Ontario
1961	Fort St. John[b]	Fort St. John, British Columbia
1962	Fresnillo	West of Fresnillo, Zacatecas
1962	La Batea	Fresnillo, Zacatecas
1964	La Honda	Fresnillo, Zacatecas
1967	Santa Cruz	Santa Cruz, Bolivia

[a] *Plan* refers to a settlement under the leadership of a bishop and is an ecclesiastically designated boundary.

[b] These settlements were not able to obtain contiguous land areas, and therefore the settlement is scattered.

[e] This settlement is nearly extinct.

Despite the friction present between the Canadian and Mexican settlements, they have been in constant contact. Most of the families that migrated to Mexico left close relatives behind, and not a single family that remained in Canada is without relatives in Mexico. Thus, much visiting back and forth took place in the years following the migration. Many "visits" to Canada became permanent. It is impossible to document accurately the return of migrants, but evidence indicates that as many as 18 per cent of each generation returned to Canada. Some estimates suggest that up to one half of the